Fail

Fail

What to Do When Things Go Wrong

Fail
978-1-5018-4783-7
978-1-5018-4784-4 eBook

Fail Leader Guide
978-1-5018-4785-1
978-1-5018-4786-8 eBook

Fail DVD
978-1-5018-4778-3

Also by Matt Miofsky

happy?

Matt Miofsky

Fail

what to do when things go wrong

Abingdon Press / Nashville

Fail
What to Do When Things Go Wrong

This book is printed on elemental chlorine-free paper.

Library of Congress Cataloging-in-Publication data has been requested.
978-1-5018-4783-7

17 18 19 20 21 22 23 24 25 26 — 10 9 8 7 6 5 4 3 2 1
MANUFACTURED IN THE UNITED STATES OF AMERICA

To my friends,
Kelli, Chris, Sara, Mike, Matt, Mike,
the ones who know me well and love me anyway

CONTENTS

INTRODUCTION

INTRODUCTION

Early in my ministry, the headmaster of a local private school reached out to me. I'll never forget what he said the first time we talked.

"Matt, I'm an atheist. But having said that, I've heard your name from several parents in my school. I would love to get together and talk."

And so we did. Every few months, Tom Hoerr and I would connect to share what we were working on, what books we were reading, what leadership struggles we were working through. Early in our relationship, Tom told me he was writing a book. Naturally, I asked him what the book was about.

"Grit," he told me.

It turns out that grit, a concept originally coined by psychologists and now fairly well known in the education field, refers to a person's ability to persevere and overcome challenges to achieve long-term goals. Grit is based on the assumption that some of our best learning experiences actually happen through setbacks, disappointments, and failures.

In the context of education, I remember Tom asking me, "Where in your life did you ever learn how to fail or how to deal with failure?"

After thinking about the question, I answered, "Sports. In sports, losing is part of the journey. You have to learn how to lose, how to grow from it, how to improve through it, and how to get back up and play another game."

He smiled and explained that a growing number of educators believe that schools must do a better job of teaching kids how to fail. And so Tom began writing about how educators can actually teach kids how to fail, especially in a culture where we are so scared of talking about or admitting failure. How do we set up instructional environments for people to fail and then learn from it? Tom told me, "Failure happens all the time. What makes you better is how you react to it."

(By the way, Tom eventually did write that book; it is called *The Formative Five: Fostering Grit, Empathy, and Other Success Skills Every Student Needs*.)[1]

Tom's idea sounds good until you try to implement it. What parents want to see their children fail? For that matter, think how frustrating it would be for any of us to learn that an assigned task never had any real chance of success—that it was assigned knowing full well that we would fail, with the purpose of teaching us how to fail well. Not many of us would feel great about that—for ourselves or for our kids.

And yet, if we look back over our lives, we know that what my friend Tom says is true. Many of our greatest lessons in life are those we learned not when we succeeded but when we fell short. I know it's true for me. I suspect it's true for you as well.

Learning how to fail is critical for our long-term success and growth. But if that's true, then it also means something else is true: if we don't learn how to fail well, then we won't ever live up to our God-created potential. If we are scared to fail and therefore shy away from anything bold, then we will leave a lot on the field of life when we are done playing.

I've seen this in other people and in myself. Some of us have not learned to respond well to frustration and failure. When that happens, we're likely to choose paths that are less risky and less challenging, in the process often destining ourselves to lives of safety, predictability, and mediocrity. By contrast, people who learn to weather some of the harshest and most tragic disappointments in life often are prepared for lives of risk-taking boldness and adventure. When we learn how to fail, we learn how to live.

So that's the idea we'll be wrestling with throughout this book—that our failures, setbacks, and disappointments have much to teach us, and God can use those lessons as seedbeds for our greatest growth. Far from being gloomy or pessimistic, a clear view of failure as a source of growth can be incredibly hopeful, even or especially for those of us currently going through hardships in our lives. What my friend Tom wanted to teach kids is something that I believe God wants to teach all of us.

In this book, we'll explore failure and the lessons we can learn from it. After all, failure is not an "if" proposition; it is a "when" proposition. If failure is not a possibility in any area of your life, chances are that you're playing it too safe and not following God's nudges. But if you're following Christ, taking chances, living by faith, loving others, or following a call, then you'll need to learn how to fail and fail well.

So rather than shy away from failure as so many people do, we're going to talk about it. We're not going to be scared by our failures or embarrassed by them. Instead, we're going to see them as occasions when God can teach us some of the greatest truths about life.

Failure is a broad topic, so we're going to focus by looking through the lens of Scripture. You might be surprised by just how flawed most people in the Bible really are. God, far from sugarcoating life or lifting up heroes who never stumble, consistently uses imperfect people, forming and shaping them as they try their best to follow God. None of them completely gets it right. All of them have moments of disappointment, and all of them learn to persevere in the midst of failure.

Of all the Bible characters who experience setbacks and disappointments and yet continue to follow God, I always come back to one person. He was a prophet, and his name was Jeremiah. As I read about Jeremiah's life, I became convinced that there isn't a guy in Scripture who has more grit. His journey has lots to teach us about how we can respond when things go wrong in our lives.

In the chapters that follow, we'll study the Book of Jeremiah—not attempting an exhaustive survey but trying to see how God worked in and through Jeremiah's failures, so we can see how God can also work through ours. Jeremiah will be like a conversation partner for us, a mentor who has experienced lots of hardships in life and has come out the other side.

Chances are that you don't know much about Jeremiah. That's okay. Let me introduce you to him.

1

JEREMIAH'S STORY

1

JEREMIAH'S STORY

In the Bible, there are two books associated with the prophet Jeremiah. One bears his name and is the second-longest book in the Old Testament. Unlike some of the other Old Testament books, it's not a simple story told chronologically from beginning to end. Instead, it kind of skips all over the place. It has poems. It has narratives. It has speeches. If you try just to sit down and read it, you may not be able to figure out the storyline. But if you dig a bit deeper, you'll see that it serves almost as a handbook for following God and remaining faithful through difficult seasons of life.

The second book is Lamentations, and it is just that—a collection of laments and poetic expressions of grief and sadness. Tradition holds that it was written by Jeremiah. Though many scholars no longer believe this to be true, most do believe it was written around the same time and under the same circumstances as those Jeremiah lived through and wrote about. It also is a raw and authentic expression of what disappointment, sadness, and despair feel like.

You may be wondering what was so bad about Jeremiah's life that he had to write a whole book of laments. Well, let me tell you a bit about the time in which he lived.

Jeremiah lived during a particularly volatile and ultimately tragic period in the history of the Jewish people. We will explore those circumstances in a moment, but for now it's enough to say that Jeremiah had a tough job, at a tough time, doing a tough task, with a tough group of people. The work didn't pan out as he thought it would, and he made a fair share of mistakes. Yet through it all, he found a way to stay connected with God, to overcome disappointments that weren't under his control, and to fight through the mistakes that were. It's fair to say that Jeremiah lived in a dark time, when it seemed that the forces of evil were carrying the day. It was a personally trying time, as Jeremiah's own faith wavered and his faithfulness often fell short.

I suspect that some of us can relate. Over the course of our lives, we inevitably hit such seasons, times when our own faithfulness flees and our belief in God waivers (or disappears altogether). We experience events that we can't control and that threaten to take us down. Like Jeremiah, we contribute to some of those seasons through our own mistakes, stupid decisions, and personal failures. But we aren't alone, and those seasons, real as they are, don't have to dictate the course of our lives. They didn't define Jeremiah. They don't have to define us.

We will encounter challenges. We will be dealt disappointments. We will make mistakes. And through our own shortcomings, or perhaps through no fault of our own, life will not always work out. Sometimes it will downright suck. We can't do anything about that. It will happen. But we get to decide how to face those moments and what to do when they hit us. We get to decide if our low points will be our last points, or if we will allow God to use those moments to reshape and remold us.

After all, it's not if you fail, but when. We will all be there. It's how we handle it that will define us.

Circumstances

Have you ever gone to a counselor, therapist, pastor, or good friend to talk about a problem in your life? If not, you should try it! If you have, then think about where a conversation like that usually begins. Where do you start? Do you jump right into the issue?

Well, I can tell you, because I sit down and talk with people all the time. No, you don't jump right in. Instead, you start off with something like this: "Well, Matt, first let me give you some background."

Have you ever done that? Whether it's having coffee with a friend or meeting with a mentor for advice, usually we set up the conversation by offering some background on the situation. We all have "background." By the way, I have noticed that usually the background phase of the conversation can last fifty-five minutes of an hour-long meeting. In the last few minutes, people finally get around to what's going on.

Why is background important? Because at any given moment, at any given time, so much of our lives is shaped and influenced by forces outside our control. The culture in which we are born, our family of origin, the decisions of those around us. We encounter natural disasters and health problems. Tragedies befall us, and friends let us down. People we depend on take off, disappoint us, or die. The economy tanks, our landlord goes bankrupt, our company gets bought, our job is eliminated, or the car we just bought gets sideswiped. I mean, there's an endless list of things that can happen to us at any time. Some of these things are day-to-day or week-to-week occurrences, while some of them are broader and more expansive cultural, political, social, or geographic realities.

Here is what's most important about circumstances. For the most part, we cannot control them. These are things that happen *to* us, *around* us, even *within* us. They are not things that happen because of us. That isn't to say that we don't bear responsibility for certain realities in our lives. But it is to say that much of what defines us and shapes us is outside of our direct control. As human beings, we can bemoan our circumstances, get mad about them, and try to control them. Or we can view them as catalysts for something new and search for ways God might be using them to shape and mold us.

Circumstances happen. How we respond to disappointing, disillusioning, or even tragic circumstances will dictate whether those circumstances ultimately bring us down or build us up. It is that choice—how to respond to circumstances—that Jeremiah must face early in his life.

Jeremiah's Context

If circumstances are important to understanding somebody's problems, then it isn't a surprise that the Book of Jeremiah starts by setting up the social, political, and religious circumstances into which Jeremiah was born and in the midst of which he would live his life.

The book starts out by placing Jeremiah in the historical context of what was happening in the Kingdom of Judah.

> *These are the words of Jeremiah, Hilkiah's son,*
> *who was one of the priests from Anathoth in*
> *the land of Benjamin. The LORD's word came*
> *to Jeremiah in the thirteenth year of Judah's*
> *King Josiah, Amon's son, and throughout the*
> *rule of Judah's King Jehoiakim, Josiah's son,*
> *until the fifth month of the eleventh year of*
> *King Zedekiah, Josiah's son, when the people*
> *of Jerusalem were taken into exile.*
>
> *(Jeremiah 1:1-3)*

The ancients often used the reign of kings to date events. If Jeremiah received his call in "the thirteenth year of Judah's King Josiah," that would be around 626 BC. He was active until at least 587 BC, about forty years later. For some of you, the dates and names may hold little interest, but stick with me.

Usually when we get these kinds of details, it's because there is meaning behind them. And in this case there certainly is.

This wasn't just any forty-year period but perhaps the most pivotal and volatile forty-year period in the history of the Israelites. The larger Kingdom of Israel had reached its height under King David, around 1000 BC. During David's reign, a belief began to emerge about God's presence in the kingdom. The people of God believed that God dwelled with them to guide, bless, and protect them. God dwelled in the country, in the Holy City (Jerusalem), and after it was built, in the Temple. All of these were tangible signs of God's presence and protection.

But around 600 BC, all that began to change. There was a growing superpower in the area, Babylon, that had the Kingdom of Judah in its sights. In 587 BC, after a long siege, the Babylonians conquered Jerusalem, destroyed the Temple, and drove most of the population into exile. What they left behind was pure desolation. God's country, God's city, God's house, and God's Temple were all destroyed. For 400 years, the people of Judah had believed that because God was with them, no one could ever conquer them. All that was over now. Jeremiah was (un)lucky enough to be born right before this happened, and his adult life spanned the period of the siege, conquest, and exile of Jerusalem and its people.

Realizing Jeremiah's historical context, we see that he was born into a looming storm—you might even say a perfect storm. If there was ever a time *not* to be in ministry, this was it. And yet there he was.

Think about it: for 400 years everything had been great, with relative peace and prosperity. Then, during one little twenty-five-year period, everything ended. And it just happened to be the twenty-five years when Jeremiah lived and worked. Talk about difficult circumstances!

But the difficulties didn't stop there. Not only was Jeremiah born at the wrong time and in the wrong place but, on top of it all, God picked him for the hardest job.

> *The LORD's word came to me:*
>
>> *"Before I created you in the womb I knew you;*
>>> *before you were born I set you apart;*
>>> *I made you a prophet to the nations."*
>> *"Ah, LORD God," I said, "I don't know how*
>> *to speak*
>>> *because I'm only a child."*
>> *The LORD responded,*
>>> *"Don't say, 'I'm only a child.'*
>>> *Where I send you, you must go;*
>>> *what I tell you, you must say.*
>> *Don't be afraid of them,*
>>> *because I'm with you to rescue you,"*
>>> *declares the LORD.*
>
> (Jeremiah 1:4-8)

I've often returned to verse 8 for personal strength during hardships. Why did God say this to Jeremiah? What did Jeremiah have to be afraid of? Well, God had just got done telling him that, from the womb, God had intentions for Jeremiah. God wanted him to be a prophet.

The Problem with Prophets

Throughout the Old Testament, there are three big jobs: king, priest, and prophet. Can you guess which job you don't want? If you're ever given those three options, don't pick prophet!

You could pick king. As king, you'd get to lead, direct, and oversee. Being a king was good. Or you could pick priest. Being a priest wasn't bad either. Your job was attending to the religious needs of the country. Priests helped connect people with God. They took care of the ritual in the temple. The priests were treated well. There are many Old Testament writings about what people were supposed to do for priests, so the priests were well taken care of and highly respected.

But Jeremiah was given door number 3: prophet. Let me tell you about prophets. Now, a prophet might sound fun and intriguing. It wasn't. Nobody wanted to be a prophet. In fact, if you go through the Old Testament, every time somebody was called to be a prophet, what did they do? They tried to bow out of the thing.

That's what Jeremiah did, right? He said, in effect, "Uh, Lord, thanks for the honor, but I think I'll pass."

And what did the Lord say? "You're gonna go where I tell you to go. You're gonna do what I tell you to do. You're gonna say what I tell you to say."

Prophet was a tough job, because prophets had to tell people hard truths. The prophets were the ones who were stoned and killed. The prophets were the ones who lived alone out in the desert. Being a prophet was not a fun job.

So Jeremiah was born at the worst possible time and in the worst possible place, and now the story says God gave him the worst possible job. God had just one more thing to do: give Jeremiah a message to share.

> Then the LORD stretched out his hand,
>   touched my mouth, and said to me,
>   "I'm putting my words in your mouth.
> This very day I appoint you over nations
> and empires,
>   to dig up and pull down,
>   to destroy and demolish,
>   to build and plant."
>
> (Jeremiah 1:9-10)

God told Jeremiah that the message would be one of plucking up, pulling down, and destroying so something new could begin.

Finally, we have all the pieces of Jeremiah's circumstances. God basically indicated that Jeremiah was to go to the king, the priests, and all the people and tell them that it was too late. They had screwed up, and there was no way to fix it. God was going to destroy everything so that something new could be created. That's a fun sermon.

It's no wonder that Jeremiah was called "the weeping prophet" or that he was long credited with writing a second book in the Old Testament called Lamentations, a whole book of laments about what was happening.

Before he even started, Jeremiah must have wondered what he had done to deserve all that. Why couldn't he have been born during prosperous times? Why wasn't he just a local priest, so he wouldn't have to worry about political events? Why couldn't he have a message of hope that God would save everyone?

It wasn't going to happen. No matter what Jeremiah did, he couldn't change his circumstances. He was born into them, and now he had to respond.

By now you may be wondering what all this ancient history has to do with you. Well, none of us may be Jeremiah, but, like him, all of us are born at certain times, in certain places, with certain challenges and obstacles. All of us have difficult circumstances, things we can't control, and realities that leave us wondering what we did to deserve this.

What's inspirational about Jeremiah is that he didn't complain about his circumstances. He didn't get mad at God. He didn't slip into thinking it was somehow all his own fault, maybe a punishment for something he did. Instead, he accepted his circumstances. He recognized that they were not his to control.

Jeremiah quickly realized that the only thing he could control was whether or not he would respond faithfully to his circumstances and trust God enough to listen. He could control whether he would shrink back and give up or lean in and step out. Jeremiah could respond with dejection or hope. As difficult as it often would be, Jeremiah responded with a hopeful insistence that God was up to something powerful even in the midst of tragic circumstances.

All of us are born at certain times,
in certain places, with certain
challenges and obstacles.
All of us have difficult
circumstances, things we
can't control, and realities that
leave us wondering what
we did to deserve this.

Our Context

Many of us are like Jeremiah. We weren't born into the middle of his mess, but we have messes all our own. Sometimes it's a mess that we create, but lots of times it just happens to us. It's part of the circumstances of our life.

Like Jeremiah, we were all born into a particular family. Some of us had great, supportive parents and a healthy family dynamic. Some of us came from homes full of conflict. Some of us had to navigate the divorce of parents. Some of us had it lots harder. Perhaps we had an abusive parent, an addict, or someone who didn't know how to show us love.

Like Jeremiah, each of us was born in a particular place with certain social and historical realities. Some of us were born into a majority population and enjoyed the benefits and relative ease that comes with such a status. Some of us were born as people of color in a majority white place, or gay in a majority straight place, or differently abled in a place where people didn't understand.

What's the point of this? It's to say that we all have context. We all have circumstances that we didn't choose that made our lives difficult, provided challenges, and perhaps even held us back from where we wanted to be.

Many of us don't have the lives we would have chosen; we have the lives we were dealt. We wish that we had different parents, that we were born in different towns, that our family had more resources, that we had a different partner or a different job. But we don't. We find ourselves with the lives we have right now.

And you know what? We may not be able to change it, but we can sure spend lots of time wringing our hands about it—wishing for this, pining for that, focusing on what we don't and can't have.

Jeremiah, as someone who has been through it himself, points us to something different, something we can control: our response.

When we are faced with our circumstances and contexts, no matter how mild or severe, we can respond in one of two ways. We can focus on our challenges and use them as excuses, or we can fight to follow God even in the midst of those realities.

In the Old Testament Book of Ecclesiastes, the author talks about wisdom and the attributes of a person who has figured out the nature of life. In that book, there is a famous section where the author talks about seasons of life. He writes, "There's a season for everything and a time for every matter under the heavens" (3:1).

The author goes on to recount life's various seasons: a time to give birth and a time to die, a time to plant and a time to uproot, a time to build something up and a time to tear something down, a time to laugh and a time to cry. These seasons may be difficult in themselves, but the most difficult part, according to the author, is that we don't get to pick them. Just as we don't get to decide that it should always be spring or that we should be able to skip the hot days of summer, we don't get to choose the seasons and circumstances of our lives.

We all have context and circumstances that we didn't choose and may wish we didn't have. But every second spent complaining about what we can't control is time taken away from what we can control. We get to choose where to go from here, how to live with the realities of our lives, and how to use those realities as fuel for where God will take us. We get to decide whether those realities will define us, whether we will use them as excuses, or whether those realities will, with God's help, propel us to be the people that God desires us to be.

Ollie

My good friends Mark and Jenn Hinkle had a son named Oliver, called Ollie, who was born with a weak heart. Ollie spent time in and out of the hospital and struggled throughout his first year of life. I had the honor of baptizing him—not in the church sanctuary as his parents had hoped but in a hospital room.

By his first birthday, Ollie's health was improving. He was gaining strength and spending more time at home. He had a great Christmas surrounded by friends and family. Then, right after the holidays, he contracted the flu and was hospitalized. The infection proved to be more than his heart could take. He went into cardiac arrest, and after about a week in the hospital, Ollie died.

Mark and Jenn were not only members of our church but also were in my small group, so I had the chance to see them bear their struggles up close, closer than most of the people I serve. I had the honor of walking alongside them during the final few weeks of Ollie's life. We had lots of time to sit and talk in the hospital over the course of the days leading up to their son's death. I got to see Mark and Jenn in the best of times and in the absolute worst.

It broke my heart to have to stand up and preach during Ollie's funeral, trying to offer words of hope in the midst of such a deep tragedy. Of course, no word, no theology, no sermon was going to change their circumstances. This was not the life they had imagined for their boy. But they tackled those circumstances with more faithfulness and courage than I have ever seen.

Over the last several years, I have watched Mark and Jenn choose hope. We don't believe that God caused Ollie to die. But our faith does proclaim that we have a God who can turn even our darkest circumstances into the seeds of new life. Inspired by Ollie's life, Mark and Jenn started a nonprofit to help the families of children with congenital heart disease. To date, they have raised hundreds of thousands of dollars, and Jenn has personally visited and stood beside dozens of other parents going through similar circumstances.

Mark and Jenn couldn't control what happened to their son, but they could control how they would respond. They could decide to trust that God is more powerful than circumstances, that God can take any conditions, no matter how bleak, and work for good.

Don't Be Afraid

The message here may not be easy, but it is simple: life is going to throw us circumstances. Some of the circumstances we cause, but lots of them are outside our control. We don't choose to have cancer. We don't choose to have horrible relationships. We don't choose to lose a job. We don't choose to have a really tough parenting role. There's lots in life that we can't control, and as humans, it's so easy to become fixated on those things.

What God gives us control over is how we respond in the middle of life's adversity. We can respond with hand-wringing. We can respond by obsessively wishing things were different. Or we can faithfully walk the road that's set before us, believing what God tells Jeremiah:

> *"Don't be afraid of them,*
> *because I'm with you to rescue you,"*
> *declares the LORD.*
>
> *(Jeremiah 1:8)*

What do we do when things go wrong? We remember not to focus on the things that we can't control but instead to respond faithfully to the task that's set before us, believing that we have a God who will deliver us. It's a lesson that Jeremiah had to learn right from the beginning of his ministry, and it's one that we must learn too.

Holy God, sometimes in the midst of circumstances, we fail to respond faithfully to the task that's set before us. So God, give us, through the power of your Holy Spirit, discernment, so that we might let go of the things that we can't control, take hold of the things that we can control, and respond faithfully, believing that you are there to deliver us. We pray these things in Christ's name. Amen.

2

THE DO-OVER

2

THE DO-OVER

As a kid, I loved to make up games. During the summer, my friends and I would spend all day outside playing, and we made games out of everything. Now, the rules of each game varied, but there was one principle that was consistent throughout all of them: the do-over.

I see the same pattern repeat with my own kids. It seems as if childhood games always include do-overs. Make a bad shot? Do-over. Get into an argument? Do-over. Someone breaks your concentration? Do-over. And it's not just kids. I've seen quite a few grown-ups on the golf course sneak in a do-over or two. (They call it a mulligan, but don't let that fool you.) It seems that we never quite grow out of the need for a good do-over.

In my own life, there are times I wish the principle applied. Words that I regret come out of my mouth? Do-over. I deeply hurt someone I love? Do-over. I get angry and do something I regret? Do-over. At one time or another, all of us have wished life worked that way, but of course we know it doesn't. Life is not a childhood game, and our behavior has real and lasting consequences.

Catching Up with Jeremiah

In chapter 1, we met Jeremiah and were introduced to the circumstances of his life. Specifically, we talked about the unique time in the Kingdom of Judah into which Jeremiah was born. We looked at his calling, the particular message he was given, and the unpopular nature of the task that was set before him. We talked about learning to cope with things we can't control.

Sometimes, though, things go wrong not because of what we can't control but what we can control. Sometimes, in fact, we experience setbacks because of things we do, such as making mistakes and choosing poorly. Unlike in a childhood game, those choices can shape our future and remain with us for years to come. And there's no do-over.

Which brings us back to Jeremiah. If you remember, the message God gave Jeremiah had a deterministic quality to it—that is, it didn't seem as if there was any way to change it. The people had sinned, and now they had to reap the consequences. It's worth pointing out that when I say they sinned, I don't mean inconsequential little one-time things.

I don't mean a little lie here, a selfish act there. The people had fundamentally abandoned God. This was sin that had been going on for hundreds of years among the very people whom God had called his own. The sin was so serious that in the Book of Jeremiah, the first twenty chapters are almost all oracles of judgment against the sins of Jerusalem. And you can boil all those sins down to one thing: spiritual idolatry.

The people had forgotten the very God who led them out of Egypt, through the wilderness, and set them up as a people all their own, in a place all their own, and gave them a country and a king and a temple. In their abandonment of God, they had turned to other things, which the Scriptures call idols. The people turned to idols for protection, meaning, and value. The idols included kings, armies, money, foreign gods, politics, and military might, to name just a few. It got so bad that the people put foreign deities up in the temple, actual statues of idols. They had cult prostitutes living inside the temple.

The people were now looking to these idols to provide what God had promised them. Tragically, the people had gone so far down this path of idolatry that it had consequences, ones that could not be changed.

God told Jeremiah that, as a result, Jerusalem would no longer be protected from the Babylonian armies—that it would fall, and the people would be taken into exile. Jeremiah had the unenviable task of sharing these consequences with the people and the king. In fact, the first part of Jeremiah's ministry would consist of futile attempts to get the leadership to hear this warning and judgment. It wasn't easy or fun. As you might imagine, it did not make Jeremiah a popular preacher. No TV deals or book signings for him. It just wasn't happening.

But Jeremiah was relentless. Over and over and over again, he preached this message: "You've failed. You've sinned. The punishment is coming. The Babylonians are coming. God is not going to stop it. You're going into exile." The way Jeremiah expressed it, there was nothing people could do to change things. It was too late. The deal was done. The pact was sealed.

You may be wondering why I'm stressing the finality of God's judgment. Where is the hope? The reason is that I think it reflects how many of us feel about our mistakes. Maybe some of you have lived really clean lives. Maybe so far you haven't made any huge errors. I admire you, I really do. But life isn't always that way, and it may not always be that way for you. I know there are others like me who have really screwed up, have made huge mistakes, have deeply hurt the people we love, or have acted in ways that are inconsistent with whom we want to be.

If you have had those kinds of life experiences, then you know that those mistakes stick with you. You almost feel as if life will never be the same. You begin to believe that your mistakes will forever shade your life and define your future, that you can never get rid of them.

That's how the people felt in the Book of Jeremiah. They had sinned, and nothing could be done about it. Their future would always be shaped by that sin, no matter how far they got away from it, no matter how much they tried to hide it. It felt hopeless.

The Potter

But then, in chapter 18, something changed. God decided to show Jeremiah something different.

> *Jeremiah received the LORD's word: Go down to*
> *the potter's house, and I'll give you instructions*
> *about what to do there. So I went down to the*
> *potter's house; he was working on the potter's*
> *wheel. But the piece he was making was flawed*
> *while still in his hands, so the potter started on*
> *another, as seemed best to him.*
>
> *(Jeremiah 18:1-4)*

This is a turning point in Jeremiah's story and in the people of Israel's collective story. This was a sign that while mistakes have consequences, and those consequences cannot be avoided, God does not abandon us. God stays with us, and God has something prepared for us on the other side. To put it more succinctly, we have to deal with our mistakes, but we don't have to be defined by them. In the midst of a dark period of life, this is a message of promise and hope.

In my effort to better understand the significance of this passage, I dropped by a local pottery shop. Pottery making hasn't changed all that much in twenty-five hundred years, so I saw something similar to what Jeremiah would have seen. I imagined I was probably the first pastor who had come up with this idea, but the potter, whose name was Ryan, just laughed. He said a few times every year some pastors who have to preach about Jeremiah 18 come by the shop for sermon ideas.

Ryan told me he had been working at the shop since he was a teenager. As a young man, he eventually bought it from the original owner and at the time of my visit had worked as a potter for decades. He had attained expert status at throwing clay. Ryan was great to show me some basics about making a clay vessel and to share some lessons on pottery.

From my conversation with Ryan, two lessons stood out. The first lesson was that, no matter how good the potter, there will be lots more mess-ups than successes. In fact, for every beautiful piece that is fit to sell, there are hundreds that never see the light of day. It's true for a beginner. It's truer for an expert. To be an expert, you have to mess up lots more!

We've said that mistakes are merely opportunities to learn and grow, and Ryan's words were a dramatic illustration of that. We often view mistakes as signs that we can't do something, aren't good enough to do something, or aren't cut out for something. We forget that mistakes are part of the journey toward expert status, whether in pottery or in life.

Mistakes can't always be avoided, but they can always be learned from. We can choose to let our mistakes define us and bring us down or to catapult us to something better. I'm not saying we should seek out mistakes—but when we make them, we need to remember that in God's hands, with a willingness in our own hearts, mistakes can help us become the people God wants us to be.

Ryan's second lesson was harder to hear but perhaps was more applicable to the passage we just read. He told me that if a pot is bad, it's easier to take it all the way down to a lump and start again rather than trying to tweak and fix it.

Mistakes can't always be avoided, but they can always be learned from. We can choose to let our mistakes define us and bring us down or to catapult us to something better.... Mistakes can help us become the people God wants us to be.

Applying this lesson to Jeremiah's story, did Jerusalem really have to be captured and destroyed? Did the nation really have to end? Did the people really have to be dragged away from their homes? I don't know that there is an easy answer to that question. But I do know that, on a personal level, we often have to hit rock bottom before we are open to change. Maybe we, like the people of Jerusalem, sometimes must be taken down to a lump in order to start again.

One of the most rewarding and gratifying parts of my job is helping people who have made terrible mistakes begin to walk the road toward reconciliation and newness of life. Years ago, I worked with a couple who had experienced infidelity. The woman had gotten close to a co-worker. They started out texting, just here and there. The texts took on a more personal tone. Then there were lunches that became more frequent and a little longer. There were after-work happy hours in which they stayed a little longer than everyone else. Then there were business trips when they had time to share what was going on in their lives, what they were struggling with, and what they were unhappy about.

You know where this is going. Pretty soon, they were making choices they knew were wrong. But somehow they justified what they were doing, convincing themselves that it wasn't so bad. The woman said that, along the way, friends tried to talk with her and point out behavior they thought was a little weird or looked suspicious from the outside. Each time, she wrote them off or told them they were blowing the situation out of proportion.

"It wasn't until we were caught," she told me, "totally and completely busted, that I woke up to the stupidity of my actions."

This revelation devastated the couple's relationship. It was also the beginning of a long, slow, and ultimately successful rebuilding of their marriage. In many ways, the marriage had a better chance of succeeding after the couple's issues were all out in the open. The marriage was reduced to a lump, and then it began to be shaped and rebuilt into something stronger.

That's the way it is with many of us. People try to warn us, give us advice, or wake us up, but sometimes it's only after experiencing the consequences of our mistakes that we are ready to submit ourselves to God to be rebuilt and shaped into something new. We often have to reach the absolute end of our own abilities and energies in order to ask for help. We often have to be totally exposed and convicted before we will finally admit that we are sinning. We often have to see the devastation our decisions have caused before we realize we need to change.

I wish this were not the case, but often it is. We have an amazing capacity to deceive ourselves and ignore the signs that we need to take a new direction. We realize how far we have strayed only when God, or someone else, knocks us upside the head.

Not the End of the Story

In the Book of Jeremiah, the indictment and judgment of Israel were harsh, and the consequences were devastating—but remember that this wasn't the end of Israel's story, just as our mistakes aren't the end of ours.

God had plans for Israel on the other side of those failures. Something new was coming. God wanted Jeremiah to observe the potter to see that when an imperfect vessel is reduced back to a lump of clay, the potter can rebuild it. This was the beginning of a message of hope for Israel and for us. God helped Jeremiah interpret what he saw:

> *Then the LORD's word came to me: House of*
> *Israel, can't I deal with you like this potter,*
> *declares the LORD? Like clay in the potter's*
> *hand, so are you in mine, house of Israel! At*
> *any time I may announce that I will dig up,*
> *pull down, and destroy a nation or kingdom;*
> *but if that nation I warned turns from its evil,*
> *then I'll relent and not carry out the harm*
> *I intended for it. At the same time, I may*
> *announce that I will build and plant a nation*
> *or kingdom; but if that nation displeases and*
> *disobeys me, then I'll relent and not carry out*
> *the good I intended for it.*
>
> (Jeremiah 18:5-10)

God asked Jeremiah a question: "Just as the potter can refashion a blemished pot into something beautiful, do you think I can take you and my people, broken and blemished as you are, and do the same?" In that moment, Jeremiah was faced with the power of God.

The idea being expressed is what theologians often call God's sovereignty. Sovereignty means the ability to do what one chooses to do without limitations from an outside force.

God's sovereignty is sometimes frightening. Does God really bring about disaster or destroy things? But sovereignty is also hopeful. There is nothing—no mistake, no consequence, no tragedy—that God cannot fashion into something new, something useful, something beautiful. No one and nothing is ever too far gone. That includes you.

This is a pivotal moment in the book, a crucial point in the story. Everything up to this point seemed set in stone: Israel had screwed up, destruction was coming, and there was nothing Jeremiah or anyone else could do about it. Jeremiah's task seemed to be simply sharing a message that had no good news in it, only the brutal reality of Israel's choices and the consequences of those choices.

But here it all turns around. God said, "Don't I have the capacity to do something new? Don't you trust that this judgment and these consequences are not the end of your story but the beginning of a new and better one?"

What about you? Do you believe that God has the capacity to refashion ruined things into something beautiful? Do you believe that God can do that with us, with our families, and with our world?

In the congregation I serve, The Gathering in St. Louis, we serve Communion every week in each of our worship services across all four of our sites. It has become a hallmark of our church that, no matter what we did or didn't do since the last time we worshiped, we come to the table to be reminded of God's power, to receive forgiveness for our mistakes, and to be reshaped into new people for a new week. Each time as we invite people to come forward and receive Communion, we say the same words: "Here at The Gathering, everyone is welcome to come and receive Communion. You don't have to be a member of this church or any church. All that we ask is that you come seeking Jesus." We serve over a thousand people Communion every week, and I personally am able to look into the eyes of hundreds of those people. Some are smiling, some look bored, some are yawning, but every weekend, a few people are crying. After worship, it's not uncommon for people to tell me that it was the day they took Communion for the first time, even though they had been coming to the church for months or even years.

It's an occasion for joy, but it tells me something else: dozens of people sitting in our church each week don't feel worthy to come forward and receive Communion, and thousands more sitting at home feel the same way about just coming to church. Somewhere along the line, many of us have become convinced that if we've messed up, then somehow we can't come to church or receive Communion. Many of us believe that our sins, mistakes, and bad choices disqualify us from God's love. When we mess up decisions, we begin to believe that we are messed-up; when we screw up our lives, it's easy to think that we are screw-ups. Beneath a veneer of success, money, a good job, and a handsome family, lots of people are trying desperately to prove themselves worthy—to their dads, their moms, their spouses, their bosses, and especially to God.

In the midst of that kind of thinking, God is saying something remarkable: "I have the power to refashion you. You don't have to prove anything to me. You don't have to be perfect to come to me. I take imperfect vessels and remold them. I take lumps of clay and form them into beautiful objects. I take messed-up people and make them new." That's what God does. If you're waiting to be good or to get your life together in order to be worthy, you may be waiting your whole life. To put yourself in God's hands, you don't have to wait. You don't have to be perfect.

You do, however, have to be one thing: willing.

Responding to God's Grace

God declares to Jeremiah through the potter story, "I have the power to change my mind and turn your destruction into joy. I have the ability to turn your failures into successes. I have the ability to break the cycle of negativity in your life. I have the power to change you."

But something is required.

> Now say to the people of Judah and those living in Jerusalem: This is what the LORD says: I am a potter preparing a disaster for you; I'm working out a plan against you. So each one of you, turn from your evil ways; reform your ways and your actions. But they said, "What's the use! We will follow our own plans and act according to our own willful, evil hearts."
>
> (Jeremiah 18:11-12)

Many see in Jeremiah's story a mean and vengeful God. I understand that view. Sometimes I read it that way as well. But from another perspective, we can see a grace-filled God. There were consequences to people's behavior, but God was still willing to change them and forgive them. If only the people would stop pretending, would turn toward God, would change their ways. If they would just show a desire to be reshaped, God was ready to do it.

The story ends in such a sad way. The people decided not to listen. They believed it was too late. They couldn't change. The consequences were set. Nothing could be done.

Some scholars believe that the people of Judah, in making this decision, were being arrogant and stubborn. But I think they were just resigned to their fate. I think they had convinced themselves that God really couldn't do anything remarkable and beautiful with them. They were basically saying they didn't believe God had the power to do a new thing in their lives.

Many of us, like the people of Judah, have resigned ourselves to our failures—to addiction, to crappy marriages, to compromised ethics, to lackluster passion. We have resigned ourselves to bad blood, broken promises, and strained relationships.

You might say, "Matt, it's no use. You don't understand what's happened in my life. There's no way I could be forgiven for the things I've done."

But Jeremiah tells us something different. Through him, God declares that when things go wrong, they can be made new again. When we finally set aside our own efforts, our own wisdom, our own courses that we're trying to run, God can begin new works in us. It begins when we say, "Okay, God, here I am; teach me something new. Take me back down to a lump of clay and then build me back up."

When we do that, God promises that something new can be created. God has the power to do that in our lives. All we have to do, according to Jeremiah, is turn around, come back to God, and make ourselves available.

We need to set aside the strategies we've been trying to use. We need to set aside the wisdom we've been living by. We need to get rid of those negative scripts we play in our heads. We need to stop telling ourselves that past mistakes define future possibilities.

We need to put ourselves in the hands of our creator, the God who says, "I have the power to turn you into something beautiful." That's God's promise to us.

Tragedy to Triumph

The people of God suffered terrible tragedy in Jeremiah's time, but God remained faithful to them. Centuries later, God raised up an anointed one from the line of David, a new king with a new kingdom. That one was Jesus.

In Jesus, we received a promise that Jeremiah longed for but saw only dimly. In Jesus, God declared once and for all that our destiny is not sin but forgiveness, not devastation but restoration, not consequence but redemption. And in Jesus, God started proving it.

God turned serving girls into saints, fishermen into leaders, tax collectors into apostles. Insignificant and flawed people were able to do incredible works when they put themselves in God's hands. Still today, God takes messed-up people and shapes them into beautiful things. God could do it then, and God can do it now.

We don't have to hide, we don't have to pretend, and we don't have to run away. Instead, we can be honest with God about who we are, where we've been, when we've messed up, what we fear, how we've failed. Then we can tell God, "I want to put myself in your hands. Fashion this lump of clay into a vessel that's worthy and able. Make me into something beautiful."

We begin where we started, with childhood games. Remember the do-over? It's true that we can't just wipe out the consequences of our mistakes; we have to live with them, often for a long time. We can't take everything back or put the score back to zero. All that is true.

But life does have do-overs. They aren't as simple as in a game. They require work and sustained effort. They involve therapy or tears or tough talks. They require humility and changed behavior. Most of all, they require turning back, abandoning our own wisdom, and replacing it with a willingness to be led by God. Our mistakes, failures, and sins may have defined our past, but they don't need to define our future. God can take us—dents, blemishes, and all—and refashion us into something new.

God, we thank you that even in a difficult story like Jeremiah's, with lots of sin, lots of messing up, and lots of judgment, there is also hope. We are grateful that it is never too late, that you are a God who has power in our lives and can do beautiful things with messed-up people like us. God, right now in the silence of our hearts, we confess to you that we are broken people, and we ask that you take us back into your hands. In Jesus, forgive us, reshape us, and mold us into something beautiful. Amen.

3

IN THE PIT

Honest about our anger toward God

Hopeful faith

3

IN THE PIT

Several years ago, my friends John and Jennifer bought their dream car. It was a red MINI Cooper. It had a double moonroof, leather seats, custom paint, and all sorts of other bells and whistles.

Have you ever bought something that you've wanted for a long time? It may be as big as a house or car or as small as a toy you wanted when you were a kid. When you finally get it, sometimes you just want to go look at it to make sure it's really yours.

The morning after purchasing the new MINI, John wanted to do just that. He woke up, got a cup of coffee, and went to peer out of his window at his new car. When he looked outside, there was his red MINI, paint glistening in the morning sun…and with a huge oak tree on top of it. Overnight there had been a serious thunderstorm with high winds, and it had pushed a decades-old tree onto John's new car, crushing the roof. Not a great way to start your day!

Now, in the grand scheme of things, it wasn't so tragic. No one had died. John and Jennifer had insurance. Everything was fixable. Though it certainly had been a gut-wrenching moment, in just a few weeks the MINI was repaired and life was back to normal.

Some low points are like that. In the moment they are awful, and we think the world is coming to an end. But in retrospect we can laugh. Why? Because the impact, no matter how overwhelming at the time, is temporary.

Other low points are much more serious and significant. Maybe you've hit rock bottom and felt that you were in a pit, something so deep and dark that you would never escape. Life can't get any lower or any worse. Many of us know what rock bottom feels like. Often that feeling is despair.

Talk About a Low Point

In the last chapter, we talked about Jeremiah and the vision God gave him through the village potter. It was a hopeful message about the power of do-overs. After years of proclaiming impending judgment, Jeremiah was instructed to offer God's people a chance to turn around and come back to God, so they could be refashioned into a new nation.

As we learned, the people refused. They chose their own way instead of God's. Even when faced with the dead-end that their own path provided, they didn't turn around. They weren't going to change, and they were tired of Jeremiah's incessant squabbling, warnings, and negativity. So finally the people of Judah turned on Jeremiah and went to the king.

> *Then the officials said to the king: "This man*
> *must be put to death! By saying such things,*
> *he is discouraging the few remaining troops*
> *left in the city, as well as all the people. This*
> *man doesn't seek their welfare but their ruin!"*
>
> *"He's in your hands," King Zedekiah said, "for*
> *the king can do nothing to stop you." So they*
> *seized Jeremiah, threw him into the cistern of*
> *the royal prince Malchiah, within the prison*
> *quarters, and lowered him down by ropes.*
> *Now there wasn't any water in the cistern,*
> *only mud, and Jeremiah began to sink into*
> *the mud.*
>
> *(Jeremiah 38:4-6)*

In the Book of Jeremiah, by the time we get to chapter 38 two political realities are important for our story. First, these were the final days for the Kingdom of Judah and for King Zedekiah. He didn't know it yet, but he would be the last real king in the line of David to rule in Jerusalem. The Babylonians were at the gate. The situation was grim and the prognosis poor. Even though God was still giving the people an opportunity to turn around, they weren't going to do it. The ship was going down, and they were going down with it.

Second, Jeremiah, as a prophet to the king, still held a privileged position within the king's court. He had access to people in power, likely including military leaders. This meant he knew they were intending to fight until the bitter end. Because Jeremiah was in the king's court, he was also expected to be supportive of the king's decisions and publicly encouraging about the situation. Remember, the people believed that no matter how dire the situation, God would protect and save them. Jeremiah, though, kept reminding them that God was not going to save the people this time. In so doing, Jeremiah was anything but encouraging. This was not a message anyone wanted to hear. On top of that, the people in power were growing increasingly concerned about his effect on the morale of those remaining in the city, including the troops. In short, Jeremiah had gone from being annoying and unsupportive to being considered a traitor, and the leaders wanted him executed.

So the officials went to the king and requested Jeremiah's execution. The king told them they could do with Jeremiah what they wished. They decided that before killing him, they would throw him into a large cistern (a pit that gathered rainwater). This may seem like an act of mercy, but it wasn't. The cistern was in a prison yard, and when someone was thrown in, they usually didn't come out. The officials threw Jeremiah in, and he began to sink in the mud.

Picture Jeremiah, a guy who had spent decades giving his life for the sake of God's call. Over and over again he had been ridiculed, derided, or ignored. He had taken on a task that had few benefits and lots of hardships. It was a job that no one else would have accepted, yet he felt called to do it because he loved Judah and loved God. And now here he was, accused of being a traitor, left to die in the bottom of a pit. It was literally and figuratively Jeremiah's low point.

You know what a low point is, right? You've been there. For some of you, it meant losing everything. For others, it meant alienating those who loved you. For still others, it meant coming to a dead-end on a path you had been traveling. For many of you, it may have been as simple as a really bad day. Whatever form it took, you probably felt like giving up. You were tired, out of options, weary of working, emotionally numb, or completely broken.

A Cool New Church

I am often asked to speak to groups of pastors about the beginning of The Gathering, the church that a group of us started in 2006. Now, when pastors go back and tell the story of their ministry, it's tempting to hit the highlights and celebrate the victories while conveniently forgetting about the failures. But when I tell about starting The Gathering, I talk about my low point.

Our vision was to start a church that would be compelling to a new generation of people in St. Louis. We had acquired an abandoned sanctuary in the city that had closed just a few months prior. It seemed like a good idea—until we began trying to renovate it. We were supposed to start weekly worship on

September 17, but the sanctuary was a disaster. We had ripped up everything but didn't have nearly enough money to put it back together. That meant that a small group of us had to work nights and weekends to do it. During that same time, I was becoming painfully aware that at twenty-eight years old, I had no real clue what I was doing. We had no band, no staff, and I was beginning to feel that whatever plan we had would be totally inadequate for the task ahead. Even if we could finish it on time, we had no idea if anyone would even come to this new church. So, what did we do? We decided to do a practice worship service to see if the pieces would come together.

As the day approached, I realized that this compelling new church was going to have its preview worship service in the musty, smelly, eighty-year-old basement of a fellowship hall. Not exactly the hippest place on earth. It was turning out to be the hottest weekend of the year, over a hundred degrees and more humid than you could imagine. Did I mention that the church didn't have air conditioning? As if that were not enough, the night before this preview worship, I got a phone call from the band. They were cancelling.

So there I was. It was Friday night. I had moved my family of four into a house that we couldn't really pay for, to start a compelling church that I wasn't sure anyone would come to, in a building that we couldn't fix up. Everything was falling apart. I was going to be lame, a failure right out of the gate. I was stressed, overwhelmed, worried about the financial stability of my family, and completely worn out. It was about 10:00 p.m. when I hit my low point. I hung up the phone, crumpled my sermon, threw it in the trashcan, and broke down crying.

That night might have been the first time in the new ministry when I felt like a complete failure, but it wouldn't be the last. God spoke to me that night, waited until my crying spell was over, and had me write a brand-new sermon. I titled it "All Great Things Begin in Garages or Basements."

The next day I shared that message, and by God's power and grace it connected. When we launched public worship for the church just a few months later, those first folks came back... with friends. We now tell that story at The Gathering as part of our new-member small group. From that low point when I felt like a failure, God was actually beginning to take over. There was something God was able to do in that place that I didn't, or couldn't, accept at any other time. As painful as that period of my life was, I look back on it with a sense of awe and gratitude.

The Lament

When Jeremiah reached his low point at the bottom of the cistern, how did he react? He prayed. It's a special kind of prayer that we call a lament, which is a cry of sorrow and sadness before God. Jeremiah's lament—even this shortened version—is a bit long, but that's the point, isn't it? He had lots to be sad about. Read his lament, and see if it doesn't resonate with how you have felt at times.

> LORD, *you enticed me, and I was taken in.*
> *You were too strong for me, and you*
> *prevailed.*

Now I'm laughed at all the time;
everyone mocks me.
Every time I open my mouth, I cry out
and say, "Violence and destruction!"
The LORD's word has brought me
nothing but insult and injury, constantly.
I thought, I'll forget him;
I'll no longer speak in his name.
But there's an intense fire in my heart,
trapped in my bones.
I'm drained trying to contain it;
I'm unable to do it. . . .
Sing to the LORD,
praise the LORD,
for he has rescued the needy
from the clutches of evildoers.
Cursed be the day that I was born.
May the day my mother gave birth to
me not be blessed.
Cursed be the one
who delivered the news to my father,
"You have a son!"—
filling him with joy.
May the bearer of that news be like the cities
that the LORD destroyed without mercy.
May he hear screams in the morning,
and the battle cries at noon,
because he didn't kill me in the womb

and let my mother become my grave,
  her womb pregnant forever.
Why was I ever born
  when all I see is suffering and misery,
  and my days are filled with shame?
                    (Jeremiah 20:7-9, 13-18)

We don't know for sure if Jeremiah spoke these words as he was sinking into the mud at the bottom of that pit or if he wrote them down later, but they express how he felt at his low point. And this probably was not Jeremiah's only lament; there's the entire Book of Lamentations, believed to be various prayers of lament from people during this same time period.

Laments are some of the oldest forms of human poetry in existence, going back to the *Iliad* and the *Odyssey*. Keep in mind that laments are not just accidental vent sessions or angry, emotional harangues. They have a very particular form and structure. Laments are carefully constructed forms of prayer that are passed down through the community. In fact, there are Old Testament scholars who specialize in studying the traditional form and function of laments. While these forms can vary widely, there are two features that are almost always present. By examining these features, we can learn more about failure, suffering, and our relationships with God.

In the first feature, a lament is honest about suffering. When people read the Bible for the first time, they often are surprised by just how honestly people speak to God. Far from sugarcoating the truth or holding back, people in the Bible let God have it! Here is Jeremiah accusing God of deceiving him.

He curses the day his mother bore him and the day his father found out he had a son. Laments are honest and raw in their emotion and anger before God.

When we think about it, haven't we all been there? Haven't we sometimes prayed a lament, asking God why something is happening to us? There have been times in my own life when I felt that even though I was doing everything God had asked of me, bad things kept happening. I've expressed my anger to God, wondered if God was listening, and been on the verge of throwing in the towel. Have you felt that way? A prayer of lament is one way to stay connected to God in the midst of anger, doubt, and pain. Laments are honest in their raw emotion.

Laments also have a second feature, and it sits almost ironically alongside the first. While laments are raw in their emotion and anger toward God, they also always include a declaration of faith. It seems strange when you read it. In the midst of a long, angry outcry to God, there will suddenly be a statement of praise and faith. We see this in Jeremiah's lament, when just before cursing his birth and his mother, Jeremiah suddenly shifts gears and proclaims, "Sing to the LORD, praise the LORD," expressing faith that God is still at work. Laments hold together this double truth: you are honestly and authentically angry, not only with others but with God, and at the exact same time, you hold onto hope that God will see you through even this.

The form of a lament may seem a bit schizophrenic, but it resonates with our experiences. In our moments of greatest doubt, we often hold out hope that maybe God is still there and will come through for us. I have been beside people at the hospital who express this double truth: we pray in anger and exasperation, yet we still believe God is good. A lament doesn't nullify the fact that we ultimately trust in God.

These two features of the lament provide insight into the way we can proceed when we hit a low point. Low points, by their nature, require a deep honesty about how much life sucks. Just sit with that for a minute. It does no good if churches, pastors, and Christians pretend otherwise or cover up hard stuff with flowery language. Sometimes life sucks. It is unfair. It makes no sense, and God seems far away. But anger toward God isn't a lack of faith; it's actually a sign that we still believe, that we trust that God is good. That's why we're so angry! Faith doesn't require that we accept the cheap platitudes that people throw our way or that we always have a smile on our face. We can let God know how we feel, even if our feeling is that God has let us down.

But at our low points, it's critical that we also hold onto some string of our faith. While we acknowledge pain and anger, we can still believe that God has a next chapter for us. We can be mad and still love God and even trust God. We do this all the time in our relationships. We can be mad at our parents and still believe they love us and want the best for us. We can be furious with our boyfriends, girlfriends, or spouses and still love them. Similarly, we can be angry with God and still sustain a deep and ultimate sense of love and trust.

Laments show us how, at low points, it's important to hold onto both feelings, no matter how contradictory they seem. If we let go of anger and refuse to acknowledge real feelings,

Sometimes life sucks. It is unfair. It makes no sense, and God seems far away. But anger toward God isn't a lack of faith; it's actually a sign that we still believe, that we trust that God is good. That's why we're so angry!

it can actually hurt our faith over the long haul. If we try to fake it before God, we risk abandoning our faith when we're no longer able to maintain our positive, smiling cover. On the other hand, if we simply vent, scream, and yell without a corresponding hope, it's easy to slip into a sense of resentment and bitterness toward God. In our low points, holding on to a deep belief in God guards us from losing our faith and replacing it with a lasting cynicism.

Several years ago I received a note from a pastor friend of mine. He's a great pastor, with a strong faith and an authentic spirit. Months before his writing to me, I had heard the heartbreaking news that he was going through a divorce. The details of the divorce were painful and messy, as they often are. His note told me that during the divorce, the hardest thing he had to do was his job! Sunday after Sunday, he had to stand up and share with people the good news of God's love, of God's enduring faithfulness, and of God's desire to do good things in our lives. My friend wrote, "It was just killing me inside. All I wanted to tell them was, 'Yes, Jesus is the answer, but he's not doing s#*& for me right now.'" You can fill in the blank.

Then my friend went on to say, "The good news, though, is that I allowed myself to feel that even though I knew in my head it wasn't true, I could feel in my heart the anger that I was experiencing in my life. In the lowest of moments I acknowledged my feelings, but managed to hold onto the faith. It would not let me go."

Honest anger and hopeful faith—we need both in order to make it through. Together they can help us weather our low points.

Fail

I'd like to think that while in the pit, sinking in the mud and cursing God, Jeremiah remembered the words that God had spoken to him at his call. Do you remember those words from the beginning of this book? "Don't be afraid of them, because I'm with you to rescue you, declares the LORD" (Jeremiah 1:8).

If you're in a pit right now, maybe you need to hear those words as well. They are true not only for Jeremiah but for you and me. They are words that God speaks over us in Jesus, that God is for us and not against us, and that God will deliver us and walk with us.

Our Defining Moments

Before we go, I have to tell you what happened to Jeremiah! It turned out that an Ethiopian eunuch, of all people, had heard about Jeremiah. He went to the king and pleaded for Jeremiah's life, reminding the king of Jeremiah's faithfulness. The king relented and ordered that Jeremiah should live. The eunuch, using rags and old clothes, made a rope that he lowered to the prophet, ultimately pulling him out of the mud and the pit. The story ends with Jeremiah coming up out of the mud, getting back on solid ground, and being restored to his place in the king's court. Jeremiah would live to see another day. His low point was not his last point.

Like Jeremiah, you will find yourself at low points in your life. For some of you, those low points will threaten to overwhelm you, even if the situations are ultimately fixable, like my late-night breakdown when I started the church. For others of you, the low points will feel like game-enders, like you don't know how you're going go on: the death of a loved

70

one, the breakup of a marriage, the exposure of a sin, the loss of financial stability. I wish I could give you a magic word for these moments. I wish I could reach through the pages and say or do something to protect you. I can't. No one can. The truth is that you'll find yourself at a low point. You may be in the midst of one right now.

When you find yourself there, remember the power of the lament and the two truths it contains. First, you don't have to pretend. You don't have to sugarcoat the truth or put a fake smile on your face in order to be faithful. You don't have to pretend in your prayers. You don't have to pretend with your friends. You don't have to pretend with your church and act like everything is okay. Most of all, you don't have to pretend with God. Like Jeremiah, we can be honestly angry, not only with others but also at God. There's something extraordinarily freeing about having a God big enough to deal with us as we really are, anger and all!

Second, hold onto hope. Know that your low point is not your last point. Whatever happens in your life, you can still choose hope. Hear that. It means there will be life on the other side of your low point. You will live to see another day. Even if you're in a hospital bed or at home with a diagnosis that threatens to end this life, God promises us there is more. Even with death, Jesus promises us that there is life on the other side.

By believing and expressing these two truths, we often find that the low points can become transformative. In them, we can attain wisdom that no book, lecture, or sermon can teach us. In fact, they can become our defining moments.

God, we thank you that you are a God big enough to hear our anger. Our faith is not always strong. Sometimes we wonder why, sometimes we don't understand, and sometimes we feel as if we have done everything we can yet still are suffering. But God, we also pray that you'd give us the knowledge to hold onto your hope, a hope that declares that our low points are not our last points, and that there is life on the other side of the pit. May we use the lessons that we learn in our low points to walk with others through the low points in their lives. We pray these things in Christ's name. Amen.

4

FINDING HOPE

4

FINDING HOPE

Warren Buffett, the famous investor and now philanthropist, writes an annual letter to his stockholders that is anticipated and read by many in the financial world. In one such letter, he offered three simple pieces of advice for investing.

1. Buy when everyone else is selling.
2. Don't buy when everyone else is buying.
3. Value, value, value.[1]

Pretty simple, right? On one level, it makes perfect sense to buy when everyone is selling and not to buy when everyone is buying. Don't we all want to buy low and sell high? As obvious as that advice sounds, it's actually the opposite of what most people do.

When things are flying high, we want to get on board. It's easy to invest in something when it's going great and all the signs are headed in a positive direction. When everyone is making money, it's easy to slap yours down and say, "Count me in." Similarly, when things are tanking and there's no evidence that anything is going to change, we want to bail. When everyone else is getting out and selling, it's really hard to pull the trigger and start buying. Yet that is precisely Buffett's advice to investors, and it's a big part of how he has become one of the wealthiest people in the world.

Buffett's investment advice points to something that's also true in our lives, especially when we're experiencing crisis: it's often during times of great chaos, in the midst of our setbacks or tragedies or disappointments, that we find our greatest opportunities for the future.

Buy Low

In the last chapter, we left Jeremiah as he was being rescued from the pit. Taken back to the king's palace, he was held as a prisoner. While there, Jeremiah found that his prophecies were beginning to come true.

The Babylonian army was laying siege to Jerusalem, and the situation grew more hopeless every day. By that time, the king had to have known that the Kingdom of Judah would not be able to withstand the powerful Babylonians. It was becoming apparent that God was not going to bail them out. The king knew that if the city fell, everything inside would be destroyed, possessions would be taken, and the leaders would be dragged off into exile. This was a low point not only for Jeremiah but for all the people of Judah. They were metaphorically in the cistern, and they were starting to sink.

It was right there, in the midst of that collective low point, that God asked Jeremiah to do something that made absolutely no sense.

> *Jeremiah said, The LORD's word came to me:*
> *Your cousin Hanamel, Shallum's son, is on his*
> *way to see you; and when he arrives, he will*
> *tell you: "Buy my field in Anathoth, for by law*
> *you are next in line to purchase it." And just*
> *as the LORD had said, my cousin Hanamel*
> *showed up at the prison quarters and told*
> *me, "Buy my field in Anathoth in the land of*
> *Benjamin, for you are next in line and have a*
> *family obligation to purchase it." Then I was*
> *sure this was the LORD's doing.*
>
> *(Jeremiah 32:6-8)*

OK, I know this is weird. Why are we reading a Scripture about some cousin wanting to sell Jeremiah a field? Well, think for a minute about the situation.

You may be old enough to remember the recession that began in late 2007. Maybe you even owned a house during that time. My wife and I had started a church just a year prior to that and had bought our first house at the peak of the bubble. We had no real income and no certainty that the church would grow to a point of financial sustainability (including a paycheck). It felt really risky to us even when the economy was good! Then the recession hit, and I vividly remember the anxiety that we and many others felt. Suddenly home values, which people had assumed would go up, started falling fast. Some owners who had to sell found that they couldn't because there were no buyers. The anxiety was palpable and heavy. It was a scary time. And the last thing anyone wanted to do was buy something they didn't need or spend money they didn't have.

If you remember that recession, it may help you understand the way things were in Jerusalem when the city was under siege. Imagine what happens to real estate prices when a foreign enemy is at the city gates, ready to sack the city, raze the buildings, and take away all of the people. You guessed it. Recession is an understatement. No one in his or her right mind would buy anything in that environment. In fact, everyone was trying to sell and get out of town before the Babylonians came over the wall.

It was in this environment that Jeremiah's cousin Hanamel came to him, ready to sell some family land. In many ancient societies, when one family member wanted to sell, other members would have a right of first refusal, and that's why Jeremiah's cousin came to him. Hanamel, like many others, was getting out of town. Selling the land made perfect sense, at least for Hanamel. But think of it from Jeremiah's perspective. Why would he ever pay money for land that was about to be destroyed? It was virtually worthless. So it must have come as a complete surprise when Jeremiah said, "I'll take it!"

> So I bought the field in Anathoth from my
> cousin Hanamel, and weighed out for him
> seventeen shekels of silver.
>
> (Jeremiah 32:9)

What's going on here? Why would God ask Jeremiah to buy a worthless field? And not just buy it but go through the very public ritual of property purchase in the ancient world: sign the deeds, have witnesses, count the money in front of other people, and register the purchase publicly. In other words, besides being a real downer of a prophet, Jeremiah was shown to be a pretty naïve money manager as well.

At this point you have to admire Jeremiah's obedience. I mean, how many of us would keep listening to God and remaining faithful? After everything that Jeremiah had been through— being mocked and derided, thrown into a cistern, left for dead, put in prison—now God was asking him to pay good money for a worthless field in front of everybody. Jeremiah couldn't catch a break. Maybe that's why they call him "the weeping prophet."

But God was not just jerking him around; there was a reason God wanted Jeremiah to buy that field and to do it in a way that everyone could see. There was a deeper meaning, and it was about to be revealed. Jeremiah didn't know it, but the purchase of that field was to be a turning point, a visible sign of hope, a declaration that God's judgment would not be Judah's final reality. Something more hopeful was coming.

Trusting and Doubting

God, speaking through Jeremiah, interpreted the seemingly irrational land purchase by offering the people a prophecy of hope:

*"The LORD of heavenly forces, the God of
Israel, proclaims: Houses, fields, and vineyards
will again be bought in this land."*

(Jeremiah 32:15)

If you've been reading this book and wondering where the
hope is, this is where it starts. Think about that statement from
God. Right at the worst possible moment, as the judgment
and consequences of sin are coming down, as enemies are
preparing to conquer the land, God proclaims a message
of hope. In a season when people are fleeing, leaving their
homes, and abandoning their vineyards, God says that this
place will once again thrive. Judgment, consequences, pain,
and suffering will not be the last word for the people. There is
a dark tunnel coming, but there is light at the end of it.

In a way, there's humor in this passage. For years Jeremiah
had brought a message of judgment and the need for repen-
tance. For years God, through Jeremiah, had warned the
people that things were worse than they thought, and the
people hadn't listened. Now, suddenly, they were starting to
believe Jeremiah. And just at that moment, God changed
course, doing a complete turnaround. Now that the people
were selling their property and leaving town, God declared
that things would thrive here once again.

What happened next was something I'm familiar with from
my own life. Jeremiah decided to go to God in prayer. If you
read the whole prayer, it's clear that Jeremiah was wondering if
God had completely lost it. Jeremiah pointed out the obvious
to God: "There are enemies at the gate, and you're telling us the

land will thrive?" The promise, while nice, was maybe not the most realistic. One author describes Jeremiah's prayer as one of "trustful incredulity."[2] I believe you, God, but also I don't. It's reminiscent of the man who told Jesus, "I believe; help my unbelief!" (Mark 9:24 NRSV).

I've been there, and maybe you have too, in that place where I believe in God but have serious doubts about what God is doing (or if God is paying attention at all). It seems absurd, but in my own life I've found myself—all at the same time— trusting and doubting, believing and not believing, having faith in God and wondering if God is even real. Especially at a low point, it can be so hard to believe that God cares and is working for something hopeful.

So I can identify with Jeremiah's prayer of trustful incredulity. I get it. But listen to the way God answers.

> *Then the LORD's word came to Jeremiah: I*
> *am the LORD, the God of all living things! Is*
> *anything too hard for me?*
> *(Jeremiah 32:26-27)*

This line really sums up the meaning of faith. Jeremiah knew what God was capable of; he had seen and experienced it. In that sense, he believed. But then, in the reality of his difficult situation, he questioned whether God could or would come through. He began to doubt that God could turn around things in his life. I don't think Jeremiah intended to doubt God's power, but that's what he was doing.

When was the last time you felt that way? I think it happens often. Many of us believe in God, theoretically. We trust God, especially when things are fine. We want to worship and follow God, within reasonable limits. But when things start going poorly, when life begins spiraling out of control and our faith is really tested, then it's a different story. We hedge our bets: "Yes, God, I believe in you, but now the situation is real and the circumstances are dire and right now I just can't afford faith. I can't just sit around, trust you, and hope things work out. I need to act. I need to find an alternate way. I need to fix this myself. Faith is fine, but this is real life."

Going back to our investment metaphor, investing hope in God during such times can feel like investing what little money we have left in a market that's crashing. Maybe it's time to sell faith and diversify our trust. Maybe it's time to invest in something new.

Then, when Jeremiah was right on the verge of quitting, God directly put the question of faith to him: "Is anything too hard for me?"

God's question to Jeremiah is one for us as well. Do you believe that the God who created heaven and earth, who parted the sea and led the people to the Promised Land, who raised Jesus from the dead and has gotten you this far—do you believe that God is real, cares about you, and has the power to do something in your life?

The point of our greatest doubt is the point of God's greatest possibility. The point when our power is running out and our hope is uncertain can also, amazingly, be the point when we depend the most on God. When we are at our wits' end, we doubt God the most and need God the most. And it's when God is able to do some of God's best work.

When we are at our wits' end,
we doubt God the most
and need God the most.
And it's when God is able to
do some of God's best work.

We see this theme throughout Scripture. When Abraham didn't know where to go, when David was on the run from Saul, when Daniel was in the lions' den, when Jonah was inside the fish, when Elijah was alone on the mountain, when Moses was completely frustrated with his task—at those moments, God's power took over and produced some of the greatest miracles of Scripture.

Remember what the angel said when Mary learned she would bear a baby, out of wedlock, with complete uncertainty about what it would mean? The angel told her, "Nothing is impossible for God" (Luke 1:37).

Ray Bradbury once wrote, "We are an impossibility in an impossible universe."[3] He was referring to the overwhelming statistical improbability that everything in the universe would turn out the way it did. And yet that's exactly what happened. Just the fact that we're here at all is a testament to God's amazing power and goodness and ability to defeat the odds.

So why shouldn't we believe that God can do another new thing in our midst, taking our present situation and turning it toward something good? After all, we're dealing with the God of creation and re-creation, and God works best when things are a mess.

Remember the Future

What God did for Jeremiah was to give him a glimpse of what was coming. This passage from Jeremiah is a bit long, but it's worth reading. Soak in God's promises, and as you read, imagine the words being spoken not only to the people of Judah but also to you.

You have been saying, "This city will be handed over to the king of Babylon through sword, famine, and disease." But this is what the LORD, the God of Israel, says: I will gather them from all the countries where I have scattered them in my fierce anger and rage. I will bring them back to this place to live securely. They will be my people, and I will be their God. I will give them one heart and one mind so that they may worship me all the days of their lives, for their own good and for the good of their children after them. I will make an everlasting covenant with them, never to stop treating them graciously. I will put into their hearts a sense of awe for me so that they won't turn away from me. I will rejoice in treating them graciously, and I will plant them in this land faithfully and with all my heart and being.

(Jeremiah 32:36-41)

With some of the earlier passages, we may think that God seems vindictive, angry, or punishing. But we should remember that we are reading one small part of a long narrative and that the story ends with hope, restoration, and new life.

Paul writes in his New Testament letter to the Romans that, "God works all things together for good for the ones who love God" (8:28). God doesn't cause our suffering, but God can work something good and new and beautiful from even our greatest suffering.

I find hope in knowing that that there is much more to my story than what I am experiencing right now. At times, Scripture gives me a glimpse of that greater story, one that always ends in good.

My former bishop, Robert Schnase, has a funny phrase that he uses: "Remember the future." When we're in our seasons of setbacks and sufferings, we must remember that there is a future for us and that God is at work in our lives.

For Jeremiah, his period of uncertainty and chaos was not the end of the story. I want you to remember that it's not the end of your story either. In our lowest moments, when others are selling, when people are fleeing, when they're saying God is not real, when all the signs seem to point downward, God invites us to double-down and invest in hope—to believe there's a bigger story that we cannot see, that we may not understand, but that is nonetheless being written by God.

Investing in hope may mean worshiping God when you feel like running away. It may mean serving someone else when you are in great need. It may mean choosing to see what you have instead of what you don't have. It may mean living as if you know that things will turn around. It may look like forgiveness or coming clean or honesty or generosity. It may mean engaging your neighborhood or community when others are saying that nothing will ever change. It may simply mean coming back to God and giving God a chance to act in your life.

Hope is not a feeling. Hope is a choice that God asks us to make. The author of Hebrews writes, "Faith is the reality of what we hope for, the proof of what we don't see" (11:1).

It's not hope if you only feel it when things are going great, if you buy when stocks are high. It's hope when you're at a low point, when stocks are going down, when circumstances give you no reason to believe, when everything seems to be crumbling. That's when God asks us to muster up an investment in hope.

Years ago I had a clergy friend who received his most challenging appointment. He was called to serve a community devastated by systemic poverty, crime, and corruption. The neighborhood was infamous as a place to avoid, as a place you wouldn't want to drive through, much less live in, unless you had no choice. I remember him saying, "Matt, I'm in the middle of a war zone. That's what it looks like."

When he said those words, I immediately thought of Jeremiah. His city had been under siege. Jeremiah literally was in a war zone.

My clergy friend continued with what I thought was going to be a complaint. Instead, he said, "But you know what? It's the best church I've ever served. We're doing great things. We're starting new ministries. The people actually care. These are some of the most optimistic people I've ever worked with, because they understand what it means to hope."

I asked, "But why? When the evidence all around them shows that things are going down, when others are saying that their community isn't worth investing in, why are they hopeful?"

He said, "It's because, as crazy as it sounds, they really do believe that God has put their best days ahead of them."

Believe it. You are not done, because God is not done. Your best days are ahead of you.

Gracious and holy God, we pray for those of us who struggle to believe that you have something good planned for us, that you can actually forgive us, that the broken things in our lives can be fixed, that something better is around the corner. May your Spirit fall upon us and hold us when we are unable to hold onto you. Help us to hope, to start living now with the joy and confidence and assurance that you have more of a story to write in our lives. We pray in the mighty name of the resurrected Christ. Amen.

5

ON THE OTHER SIDE OF EXILE

5

ON THE OTHER SIDE OF EXILE

J. R. R. Tolkien wrote in *The Lord of the Rings*, "Oft hope is born when all is forlorn."[1]

Even if you have never read the book or seen the movie, you can probably guess the context of the quote. Things are not looking good for the Fellowship of the Ring, the forces of evil seem to be winning, and the outcome of the conflict seems inevitable. That is when Legolas speaks these words.

Tolkien's Christian faith is well known, and throughout his writings there are themes of faith embedded in the story. This one quote sums up so well what we Christians believe about life—that it is often at our lowest moments when something new begins. We cannot always see the new beginning, but it is there.

Our lowest point is often a seedbed for something new and better to take root and begin growing. In due time, we are able to look back and see that our lowest point was in fact our defining moment. For that reason, we have hope even in the midst of life's dark seasons.

This truth is demonstrated throughout Scripture, but nowhere is it so decisively claimed than in the resurrection story of Jesus. I love that the resurrection story in John begins with Mary Magdalene going to the tomb: "Early in the morning of the first day of the week, while it was still dark... (20:1a)." The greatest story of new life, hope, and God's power to defeat evil and death begins at the lowest point, "while it was still dark." No one could see it, but God was doing a new thing that was about to be revealed. The same is true in the story of Jeremiah.

God Was Not Done

By now, the situation in which Jeremiah lived and carried out his ministry should be familiar. Over decades, Israel sinned and turned away from God, God warned them, God gave them an opportunity to repent, they refused it, Jeremiah and other prophets warned them to turn back to God, they continued to refuse, and then judgment finally had come in the form of the Babylonian army. Eventually, the city of Jerusalem—along with the temple—was besieged, sacked, and destroyed. The people's confidence in their God was shaken as they were dragged off into exile. Judah, the last vestige of Israel, was utterly destroyed. Jeremiah had turned out to be right, but there was no glory in it. He, like the rest of the people, was left broken, devastated, and exiled from the land he loved.

The story of Jeremiah is a difficult one; there is no doubt about it. It represents the ultimate low point for God's people. So much of the Old Testament was written or edited during that time and through the lens of those events. Those decades would come to define so much of the future for God's people, and those events had ripple effects that are still felt today. With all of this, it's easy to view the Book of Jeremiah as tragic—worth reading but not worth dwelling on. After all, in a world that is currently experiencing brokenness, division, violence, and injustice, we need stories of hope. We don't need stories of sin, judgment, and despair. I understand why many people skip over Jeremiah, preferring instead an uplifting psalm or an encouraging word from Jesus.

But before you give up on Jeremiah, remember that the story does not end there. Hidden in the darkness, when all seemed lost, was the beginning of something new. God had not abandoned the people, and the future would eventually be brighter than ever. God was not done with Jeremiah quite yet. In their darkest season, the people of Israel would begin to experience incredible hope. So let's take a look at the end of Jeremiah's story.

Sitting in the occupied city of Jerusalem, before being taken away, Jeremiah penned a letter to the elders of Israel who had already been captured and taken off to exile in Babylon.

> *These are the words of the letter that the*
> *prophet Jeremiah sent from Jerusalem to the*

> *remaining elders among the exiles, and to the*
> *priests, the prophets, and all the people, whom*
> *Nebuchadnezzar had taken into exile from*
> *Jerusalem to Babylon.*
>
> *(Jeremiah 29:1 NRSV)*

Up to this point, I've mentioned exile, but now let me explain it. Exile was a war policy and strategy of the Babylonian Empire. Instead of simply destroying the land and killing the people or trying to rule them, Babylon took the most able and powerful people away from their homes and resettled them in a foreign land. The Babylonians reasoned that this would make conquered lands easier to rule and subdue, since no one but poor peasants were left behind. It was a cruel and devastating form of occupation, and it was now happening in Jerusalem. It began in 597 BC and would continue until the final destruction of the city in 587.

Historically, exile not only was meant to subdue a country but also to break down the will of the people. It subjugated them not only physically but also emotionally and spiritually, through acts of isolation and separation. Exile was synonymous with alienation, loneliness, and hopelessness. That's what exile felt like to the people who were experiencing it. They didn't know how long it would last or if the feelings would ever go away.

Some of you might feel that you're in exile. When we are in dark periods of our own, we can feel isolated, far away from others. We can feel like foreigners even if we're at home. We are left wondering how long the dark period will last or if life will ever feel good again. We may long for earlier, simpler, and happier times. In exile it's easy to give up hope. In exile we have to wait—for healing, joy, clarity of direction, and signs of hope. Exile can mess with our identity. It can make us feel like a different person, longing to get back to the one God created us to be. If you've ever felt any of these things, then you can identify with the elders and officials of Judah, the ones to which Jeremiah was writing his letter.

Settle In and Start Living

You might expect Jeremiah to rub it in and say to the elders, "I told you so!" But he didn't. Instead, surprisingly, in that darkest period Jeremiah's words began to turn hopeful. The worst was happening, but the story was not over. Far from the words of warning and judgment that marked most of his career, Jeremiah's words were of restoration and hope.

> *The LORD of heavenly forces, the God of Israel,*
> *proclaims to all the exiles I have carried off*
> *from Jerusalem to Babylon: Build houses and*
> *settle down; cultivate gardens and eat what*
> *they produce. Get married and have children;*
> *then help your sons find wives and your*
> *daughters find husbands in order that they too*
> *may have children. Increase in number there*
> *so that you don't dwindle away.*
> (Jeremiah 29:4-6)

Essentially, Jeremiah told the people in exile to settle in and start living, because they would be there awhile. It was not what most of them probably wanted to hear. I'm sure they were praying and hoping that at any minute the Babylonians would change their minds and let them go. Besides, settling in and starting to live seems dangerously close to acquiescence, and refusing to settle down could have been viewed as a form of protest.

Instead, Jeremiah had a different message: "Live where you are. Don't wait for things to improve before choosing to feel better and live differently. Build houses, get married, have kids, plant gardens. You can't control your circumstances, but you can control your responses."

Jeremiah's words have lots to offer us, especially when we are in our dark seasons, our mini-exiles. At The Gathering, for example, three of our sites are near two major universities in St. Louis. As a result, we have many undergraduates, graduate students, residents, and other university people attending our church who plan to be in the city only for a specified period of time. They are transient, just passing through.

I've noticed that, over time, these people react to their transient status in two different ways. Some will never quite invest. After all, they don't plan to be here long. They don't want to get involved in community organizations, they resist dating, they don't get too close to friends, and they may show up to worship but don't want to commit to anything beyond that. As a result, the city never quite feels like home.

Others react completely differently. Knowing they are not here long doesn't stop them. Instead, they decide to soak up their experiences. They get involved, find churches, begin serving, make friends, and get to know the neighborhoods where they live. They plant themselves and grow roots, because it's a better way to live. I've seen this attitude change people reluctant to be in a new place and turn them into passionate advocates of their new city. Meanwhile, the reluctant ones often are unhappy with their transient home for three or more years, in part, because they never allow themselves to get connected.

The same thing can happen with emotional exile. There's a temptation to stop any forward progress when things are not lining up the way we want them to. It becomes hard to invest ourselves in anything. You may know this feeling. Maybe you've experienced the exile of loneliness, depression, addiction, or loss and have allowed a paralysis to set in. Something as simple as getting out of bed can be difficult. You may neglect friendships, refuse social opportunities, stop exercising, and sink further into exile. If so, you are not alone. Many of us have been in that place. I've been in that place, and so has Jeremiah.

Don't allow your circumstances to stop you from investing in life. I know this is more easily said than done. Sometimes it takes help—counselors, friendships, daily disciplines, and an extraordinary level of courage. But Jeremiah urges us, even in exile, to keep living and resist the temptation to stop, because God is not yet done.

The Disciplines of Exile

Then Jeremiah gave perhaps the most confusing piece of advice yet:

> *Promote the welfare of the city where I have*
> *sent you into exile. Pray to the* LORD *for it,*
> *because your future depends on its welfare.*
> (Jeremiah 29:7)

In other words, he was encouraging them to pray for the very people who had captured them and taken them into exile!

At first, Jeremiah's advice sounds profoundly unfair, oppressive, and unjust. But, as we have seen, prayer is a way of staying engaged with God in the moments when we most want to turn away. Prayer guards us from a cynicism and resentment that could threaten to consume us, especially in a period of exile. Prayer orients us toward God at times when we might be tempted to pull away. As we saw earlier with the laments, prayer doesn't have to be pretty; it doesn't have to sugarcoat reality. Even our tough, honest, authentic prayers keep us oriented toward the God who is not yet done with us.

Jeremiah's words echo a familiar passage in the New Testament. Do you remember what Jesus said we should do for our enemies? He commanded his followers to pray for them. If any of you have ever been hurt deeply by another person and had to go through the process of forgiveness, one of the most difficult and powerful spiritual exercises is to do what Jesus teaches. One of the last steps in forgiveness—a sign that you're turning the corner in a relationship with someone who has hurt you—is to pray for the other person's welfare. This does not condone what they did or allow them to continue acting in your life. Instead, prayer is a way of taking power back in a situation where you feel powerless. Jeremiah reminds us that we are not powerless; we can pray for the things that we want to see changed.

Growing roots where we are planted, investing in life even when we are hurting, refusing to allow circumstances to paralyze us, working through processes of forgiveness, praying for the people who have hurt us—these are the disciplines of exile. We won't always be able to practice them, and there will be times when we are not yet ready, but they are Jeremiah's wisdom for those in places of exile. These are disciplines that help us move from darkness to light. These are ways for exiles to take back power, resist passivity, actively hope, and stay connected to the God who is not absent, and who is not yet finished with us.

Don't Listen to the Lies

Hope is coming. But before it arrives, Jeremiah gives us one more warning, and in my experience, it may be the most important.

> *The LORD of heavenly forces, the God of Israel, proclaims: Don't let the prophets and diviners in your midst mislead you. Don't pay attention to your dreams. They are prophesying lies to you in my name. I didn't send them, declares the LORD.*
>
> *(Jeremiah 29:8-9)*

Historically, here is what was happening: There were prophets preaching and teaching resistance, violence, revolt, and even war popping up among the exiles. They wanted Judah to keep fighting. Jeremiah saw a different way. He believed the way through exile was not by returning to what got them there in the first place but by returning to God, the only one who could get them out. Jeremiah reminded them that while in exile, there would be many who would whisper and shout lies, and that in our low points, we are especially susceptible to false prophets.

I've seen this in my own life. When I'm hurting, I tend to be susceptible to two particular lies. The first lie is this: "Because things are not good in your life right now, you might as well go ahead and do _____." You fill in the blank. In other words, when we're hurting, it becomes so easy to rationalize self-destructive behavior.

As part of my ministry, I talk with many people, particularly guys who feel as if they have no one else to talk with. Many men want to make it look like they have it all together on the outside. They project success or strength or a great family life when, behind the scenes, they may be dissatisfied with their jobs, trapped in their obligations, or disconnected in their marriages. It's an exile of sorts, and if one spends enough time in that place, decisions that we know are wrong suddenly begin to look okay. Maybe we fly off the handle at home, taking out our anger on the people we love. Maybe we cut a few corners with money. Maybe we begin spending a little extra time with someone from work. Maybe having a few drinks in the evening seems perfectly normal.

That first lie essentially seeks to take us down. The second lie seeks to keep us down. Here it is: "You've done something messed-up, so you are messed-up." To put it differently, when we're at a low point, we can begin to believe that it's what we deserve, that our situation is beyond changing, and that where we are is where we will always be. We can start to see our situation not merely as a consequence of what we have done but as a definition of all we will ever be. In this way, our mistakes and their consequences can threaten to define who we are, what we are capable of, and what is possible in the future. We forget the power of God to do something new in us, and we begin to believe that exile is the final chapter of our story.

Jeremiah, in his wisdom, reminds us not to listen to lies that will be whispered in our ears when we're in places of exile. When we're most vulnerable, we will be tempted to listen.

God Has Plans

But if we don't believe those lies, then what should we believe? Jeremiah answers that question with the most powerful and most quoted words of the entire book.

With those words, Jeremiah gave the people of God something to replace the lies with, a mantra to repeat while they were in exile, a hope to cling to when life was hard. With one verse, Jeremiah made all the tough words of judgment and all the harsh prophecies worth it.

> *I know the plans I have in mind for you,*
> *declares the Lord; they are plans for peace, not*
> *disaster, to give you a future filled with hope.*
> (*Jeremiah 29:11*)

God is for you, always and
everywhere....Jesus' death and
resurrection was the ultimate
statement that God will go
to the ends of the earth,
the depths of hell, and the
heights of heaven for you.

If you ever had to memorize Scripture, this one probably made the list. It's the most recognized passage in all of Jeremiah and has been etched all over cheesy Christian art. But it is repeated for a reason. It's the most hopeful verse in Jeremiah and likely one of the most hopeful in all of Scripture. It declares what God is like, what God is doing, and what happens on the other side of exile.

Take a moment and notice a few things about that verse. First, it starts with an emphatic *I*. God declares, "I know the plans I have for you." We may not know what is coming. We may not know what is next. We may wonder if there's light at the end of the tunnel. We may be uncertain, but Jeremiah reminds us that God is not. God knows the plan. God has a future in store for us. God is absolutely clear about what is coming. And we are invited to rest in that hope, because God does know.

The second thing to notice is the emphasis on welfare rather than harm. During exile, it can feel sometimes as if God doesn't care, or worse, that God actually wants us to suffer. Here, God sets the record straight, reassuring the people that it's their welfare God is after.

Friends, if you take anything from this entire book, this is it. God is for you, always and everywhere. God desires your welfare. What God promised through Jeremiah, God made good in Jesus. Jesus' death and resurrection was the ultimate statement that God will go to the ends of the earth, the depths of hell, and the heights of heaven for you. Sin, mistakes, tragedy, pain, suffering, and even death, while real, are not final. God has an endgame, and it is our welfare, not our harm. Whatever payment you think God requires from you, "he canceled it by nailing it to the cross" (Colossians 2:14). In its place, God has declared that your future is life and hope. When we are in exile, those words are a lifeline. Hold fast to them.

Finally, notice what God is giving the people, and by extension all of us. God is working to give "a future filled with hope." I read a book recently that contrasted hopefulness with hopelessness. Hopefulness, according to the author, stirs imagination, expands horizons, influences events, energizes, and creates a sense of buoyancy. Hopelessness shrinks the radius of possibility, becomes apathetic, entraps, minimizes options, resigns to existing conditions, and loses heart. Hopefulness, my former bishop might say, remembers the future so that we will not remain trapped in the present.[2]

In the Bible, Jeremiah follows God's pronouncement about hope with these inspirational words:

> When you call me and come and pray to me, I
> will listen to you. When you search for me, yes,
> search for me with all your heart, you will find
> me. I will be present for you, declares the LORD,
> and I will end your captivity. I will gather you
> from all the nations and places where I have
> scattered you, and I will bring you home after
> your long exile, declares the LORD.
>
> (Jeremiah 29:12-14)

The end of Jeremiah's story is as ironic as it is fascinating. The Babylonians that he feared so much actually gave him a choice of where to live. He decided to take off for Egypt, where he likely died. His secretary, Baruch, recorded his words. But in the end, the events in Jeremiah's life weren't the key; the important thing was his message. God chose him to speak words that reverberate still today with all of us weary exiles.

Concerning the people of Judah, everything Jeremiah said came true. They served their term in exile, and then, at the appointed time, God lifted up someone to free them. They were allowed back to Jerusalem, and they rebuilt the city walls and the temple. Ultimately, the story of Jeremiah set up the expectations that surrounded Jesus at his birth.

Those of you who know the story of Scripture can see that in Jesus, early Jewish Christians saw the ultimate fulfillment of Jeremiah's promise. God raised up a leader, but he turned out to be fundamentally different from other leaders. This leader oversaw a kingdom that would have no end. He would establish a kingdom open to all, irrespective of mistakes. He would settle, once and for all, every single one of our sins, take care of our punishments, and erase our debts. His followers have the freedom to live in love, joy, hope, and life.

As we end, you might be in a tough spot right now. Maybe you've been through the pit and you have lived to tell about it. Maybe you've been to the land of exile for a long time—weeks, months, even years—and you are back to testify that there is a future. Some of you have life circumstances that are overwhelming and are threatening to sap any shred of joy and hope that you have. Some of you are living with the consequences of mistakes and sin. Others of you have a sense that such consequences are coming.

Wherever you are, know this. We are human, and on this side of heaven everything will not always work out. We will fail. We will fall. We will make mistakes. We will hurt people. We will be hurt and find ourselves in situations that are not of our making. We will suffer at times and go through dark periods. We will lose people we love. Marriages will not always work out, finances will not always be great, job satisfaction will not always be high, and fulfillment will not always be felt. We will have setbacks and disappoints, and life will not always go the way we had imagined. This is part of life. It's going to happen, but it's not the end of our story. God is not finished. Our low point is not our last point. In Jesus, even now, God is working for our welfare and not our harm, to give us a future with hope.

Maybe a fitting way to close is with the same invitation that Jeremiah offered to the people of God thousands of years ago. Maybe, like them, we've been trying to do life on our own, ignoring God's wisdom, and pursuing our own goals. Maybe we've been relying too much on our own abilities to get through life, managing money, career, marriage, meaning, friendship, and significance.

Maybe what we need is Jeremiah's invitation to repent, turn around, and focus our eyes and lives on God. We can do that by following Jesus Christ. Try it. Test God, and see if God in Jesus doesn't produce promise, hope, and joy, even in the midst of your most trying times.

Gracious and holy God, pour out your Holy Spirit that brings us hope even in the midst of exile. God, help us to know that in

Christ you cast your ballot for us and not against us. In Christ, you proved that you want our welfare, not our harm. In Christ, you showed that forgiveness comes on the other side of judgment, and that you are giving us a future with hope. Help us to believe this, hope in this, and live this. For all of us who are in exile from you, living life on our own terms, may today be the day we turn back. As we take that step back toward you, take a step toward us. This day we commit ourselves to you; in the name of Jesus Christ our Lord. Amen.

NOTES

Introduction

1. Thomas R. Hoerr, *The Formative Five: Fostering Grit, Empathy, and Other Success Skills Every Student Needs* (Alexandria, VS: ASCD, 2013).

4. Finding Hope

1. Brad Tuttle, "Warren Buffet's Boring, Brilliant Wisdom" *Time*, March 1, 2010. http://business.time.com/2010/03/01/warren-buffetts-boring-brilliant-wisdom/.

2. Walter Brueggemann, *The Role of Old Testament Theology in Old Testament Interpretation: And Other Essays* (Eugene, Oregon: Cascade, 2015).

3. Bradbury, Ray. "World Hunger," PBS, January 27, 1975.

5. On the Other Side of Exile

1. J. R. R. Tolkien, *The Return of the King: The Lord of the Rings Part Three* (New York: Mariner Books, 2012. First published 1955 by George Allen & Unwin, Ltd).
2. Peter Steinke, *A Door Set Open: Grounding Change in Mission and Hope* (Herndon, VA: The Alban Institute, 2010).

ACKNOWLEDGMENTS

After my first book, people asked me how it felt to be a "writer." I often reply that, just as there is a difference between someone who plays golf and a "golfer," so is there between someone who writes and a "writer." I am someone who writes. There are a lot of people around me who help shape my words, thoughts, and stories into something worthy of a writer.

All of us fail, including pastors. We cannot learn and grow from our shortcomings without great people around us. My friends have helped me to do just that. They know me well and love me anyway.

I am grateful to the wonderful people I work with, and for, at The Gathering. An incredibly gracious staff and congregation, they allow me to learn how to be a pastor on their watch. I am so grateful for the affirmation, encouragement, and correction I receive from people who listen to me preach and read what I write.

I am grateful to the staff at Abingdon Press, especially my editor Ron Kidd, who patiently works with me as I stumble and fumble my way toward becoming a writer.

I am grateful for my three kids, Caleb, Carly, and George, and my wife Jessica. They have seen all the ways I have fallen short, but together we continue to grow as a family. I love you all!

Finally, I am grateful to God in Christ, who has saved me from all sorts of sins, mainly of my own making, and given me a calling to teach and serve in the church. It is a high calling that I try to live up to more and more each day. For anything in this book that is helpful and life-giving, thanks be to God who is endlessly forgiving and gracious to all of us—you and me included.